ALLEN AND WIN32

AN UNFINISHED JOURNEY

OMPRAKASH

I DEDICATE THIS BOOK TO MY PARENTS AND FRIENDS.

Contents

Preface

Allen is more of a child prodigy to say the least. He loves to read and has a inqusitive nature about everything he come across right through his academic career. But it continued even in his professional career also. How he overcomes all the obstacles and became unique.

Prologue

Well , i have been pondering to write short stories for a long time. I have written numerous poetry books. They are Senile god Act 2.0, Yours Truly and First Thought Of God. I decided to write "Allen and win32" as a series . Not much to say . KIndly provide continous support all through out the series.

CHAPTER ONE

chapter 1

Allen was then joined chemical engineering in coimbatore. He really was a mediocre student. He still has continous passion to find out how things would have invented or formed or created. This continued till now for him. But now in a far more matured way.

Well he wants to do computer sscience engineering but his mother suggested or rather i would say in a way forced him o pursue chemical engineering . at that point of time, allen was dejected but immediately he pulled himself and convinced his mother that he would to do a computer course which will make him to take a career in software.

he arrived chennai morning to discuss with his parents about change of engineering discipline. And it turned out to be compromise ,he immediately took west coast train to coimbatore after having spent just four hours with parents . All his friends wondered that how come you not even spent a day in chennai and returned immediately.

now then during his second year in coimbatore institute of technology he studied voraciously . both chemical and software course. his urge to understand everything in life make him to grow as an eccentric personality. his friends has other thoughts about him. but his continous urge to find how things would have born, even for trivial things. He prefers to know, what and all went in the mind of inventor made him to invent an entity. Tthose thoughts are not even possible,by the inventor . But his obsession grown so much that the concepts taught in classes were not enough. so he did lot of thought experiments and when semester examination appeared he prepare for the sake of marks or grade. which he did not like. All four years of study in coimbatore institute of technology went like that . The peak of the confusion leads to erratic behaviour. his thought experiments continued in the campus interview. he would have got the job effortlessly . his quench to understand everything leads to experimentation even before the interviewer. hence he was not selected.

he felt dejected and thrown tantrums. it is after that allen started understanding thngs so nicely wich he did not share with his friends from then on his academic life was a relishing one. most of them thought that allen was a failure. but allen never bothered about that.

CHAPTER TWO

Earlier allen prefere to take GATE. But after his failure in campus interview following which he understood all those technical jargons and concepts much easiuer than before. he decided that GATE was not much competitive and so he prepared to take GRE , hence he prepared wordlist voraciously. and he hence moved from first row to the last row in the class.

all his professors were little upset about his behaviour or rather felt slightly that he became disobedient. Not listening to the classes.

Also not efficient in laboratory experiments. even his friends also thought that way. but inside him, his confident level in academic grown so much but he didn't showed it to others including his beloved friend and guide which happened to be his fahter.

He graduated in the year 1998. now after graduation he waited for GRE results. but the score was not encouraging one. He again joined another computer course following which he got employment in mind and brain systems. there he became workalholic.

His immediate manager seeing his hardwork of allen that whether he would stay or leave after performance appraisal. he appeared rebel meaning he solve whatever the problem could be . his knowledge hunger grown so much that he read voraciously . the stage has reached where he started buying books once in a week and finish them in a day or two . The reading could have been a shallow read or in other words it was skim through.

Now again becaus of break-free hardwork he became ecccentric and lost his job.

CHAPTER THREE

After he left the job he decided to have two objectives. one was a short term goal to get a master in computer science in MIT. Another was a long term which is to win NOBEL PRIZE .

Now then he felt that his thirst in information technology was over. he finished the syllabus of M.S.(Computer Science) on his own. Now he turned his attention towards to other engineering discipline as well. He sustained his reading habit be it fiction or technology books. over a period of time it so happened that his metaskill grown so much that he could crack any problem given a time frame.

As years passed, allen decided incidentally to start writing poems. His first few poems are "temperature", "birds", and "servant"..He was so astonished that it came out as a nice entity. and so he continued his writing . initially he used to write ten or more poems. now more than a decade went his writing poetry matured so much that he received encouraging words from critics as well.

CHAPTER FOUR

WinMain() was one of the first windows APIs. Also happened to be allens's first known API in windows. And first book he heard for windows programming was "charles petzold". The year he heard about windows programming was 1997. At that time , when he saw that book, he got totally frustrated. That book is more than one thousand two hundred pages. it really was far reaching for him to complete it.

Then after finishing his graduation he joined "mind and brain systems" . It happended by coincidence that he has to come across that book which he saw during 1997. This time he has better edge over last time.

During his college days, to finish a page of a book, it took long hours. But during mind and brain he has grown so much that he could complete a book in fewdays . He started reading voraciously and his first WIN32 API in win32 programming by charles petzold was "WINMAIN()".

He really got motivated to complete this book as early as possible . But he dont want to complete in a fast pace. He relished the content of the book ,whether he understand or not. He just cultivated a habit of go through any book by skim through method. when he saw Registerwndclass() it took him into different maze , from which he couldn't come out . Not only above apis, but also HINSTANCe, hprevinstance and ncmdshow so on. All he knew from prior experience was they are arguments or parameters.

Well, well, well, it was a monumental effort to understand chapter 3 of that book. Before that there was hungarian notation and also about unicode. who would understand ,ofcourse person of his calibre found out so hard.

Now then he decided to skim through that book again after unicode. It had keyboard , mouse, menus, dialog boxes, control APIs. Ofcourse document - view architecture and multithreading and networking and so on.

End Of Allen And Win32 :volume 1

Volume 2 is about to come. Stay connected . kindly provide feedback to sbaktavatshalam@gmail.com.